Ron Fry's

HOW TO STUDY
Program

Take

Notes

By
Ron Fry

THE CAREER PRESS
180 Fifth Ave.
PO Box 34
Hawthorne, NJ 07507
1-800-CAREER-1
201-427-0229 (outside U.S.)
FAX: 201-427-2037

Ron Fry's HOW TO STUDY Program: Write Papers
ISBN 0-934829-91-8, $4.95

Cover design by Dean Johnson Design, Inc.

pp. 84-89 excerpted from **FROM CAMPUS TO CORPORATION And the Next Ten Years** by Drs. Stephen Strasser & John Sena. Copyright © 1990 Drs. Strasser & Sena. Reprinted with publisher's permission.

Copies of this volume may be ordered by mail or phone directly from the publisher. To order by mail, please include price as noted above, $2.50 handling per order, and $1.00 for each book ordered. Send to: The Career Press, Inc., 180 Fifth Ave., P.O. Box 34, Hawthorne, N.J. 07507

Or call Toll-free 1-800-CAREER-1 (in Canada: 201-427-0229) to order using your VISA or MasterCard or for further information on all books published or distributed by The Career Press.

Table of Contents

Ron Fry's
HOW TO STUDY
Program

Take
Notes

Take Note: And Improve Your Grades!

Quick, what was the worst class you or one of your friends ever suffered through?

For me, that's an easy one. It was my friend Tony's eighth-grade American History class with Sister Anne Francis. And it was a note-taking nightmare.

Each day, the good sister filled—twice—all eight blackboard panels in the classroom with names, dates, places, wars, rebellions and treaties—more facts than there are tombstones in Arlington Cemetery. And the students sat there, silently copying *every word* into *their* composition books.

They even had to be careful *how* they copied. Their penmanship was expected to be just as perfect as Sister

Anne's; if it weren't, their grades suffered. (She checked their notebooks once a week!)

They were assigned no reading and no homework. It wasn't until near the end of the semester that Tony found out why. He discovered a textbook ostensibly assigned to the class on a back shelf—which the good sister was merely copying, word for word, every day, onto the blackboard! And which the students dutifully copied, word for word, into their notebooks.

That seems like a useless exercise, doesn't it? When all the teacher had to do was just pass out the text!?

Unfortunately, the methods most of you are using to take notes are probably not much more useful.

With one difference—here's the book.

The pitfalls of poor note-taking skills

While most of you will have the good fortune *not* to sit in a classroom commanded by an obsessed nun, too many of you will still develop severe cases of writers' cramp in crazed efforts to get down every single word your teachers utter.

Others will take notes so sparse that, when reviewed weeks—or merely hours later—they will make so little sense that they might as well have been etched in Sanskrit.

Taking poor notes—which can mean too *few* or too *many*—will undoubtedly mean poor results—lousy grades and loud lectures from parents, with frequent references to "your future's going down the drain," "low-paying jobs" or "on the beach"...bum.

If you feel compelled to take down your teacher's every pearly word, or recopy your entire text, you certainly won't have much of a social life—where would you ever find the time? Maybe you're so horrified at the prospect of *reliving* those hours of lectures and chapters of text that you simply *never* review your notes. And if you skip note-taking altogether...well, I don't need to tell you what kind of grades you should expect.

Note-taking should be the ultimate exercise in good old American pragmatism. You should take notes only on the material that helps you develop a thorough understanding of your subject...and get good grades, of course. And you should do it in a way that is—first and foremost—useful and understandable to you. A method that's easy to use would be a real plus.

Most students have a difficult time developing a good note-taking technique and recognizing the information that always shows up on tests—an understanding of which is essential for good grades.

Failing to learn good note-taking methods, they resort to what *I* think are useless substitutes, such as tape recorders and photocopying machines.

There is a *right* way to take notes

In this book, I will present the essentials of a note-taking system that works for me and, I'm sure, will work wonders for you, too. This was not a skill that just came to me, full-blown, in a dream one night, but one that developed over the years—in high school, college, and on the job as a writer and editor. In the chapters ahead, you will find the distillation of that experience.

And you'll discover that my tried-and-true system is one that is not only easy to learn and *inexpensive,* but one that you can begin using *immediately*—whether taking notes in class, studying a textbook or another reading assignment, gathering information for a term paper or preparing for an exam.

What's in it for you?

What are the benefits to you when you learn to take better notes? This book will not only help you become better at writing down essential facts, it will help you improve your *listening* skills. And guide you toward the path of real learning, rather than just learning how to memorize and repeat names, dates and factoids.

Good note-taking skills will put you in greater control of your time and provide you with a better way to organize your student life. You'll no longer find yourself spending long hours filling notebook after notebook with redundant material, just so you can spend hours rereading it all later. Nor will you ever again need to pull "all-nighters" just before a big test on a subject that you have inadequate notes for.

At test time, you will have the essentials of your class and homework assignments at your fingertips—review will be a breeze.

When you have to research and write a paper, you will have a method that helps you utilize your time in the library and organize the information you gather there more effectively and efficiently. Preparing your reports will be a snap.

But developing your note-taking skills will reap benefits for you much further down the road as well. The ability to listen effectively and glean the most salient information from a meeting, speech or presentation will be a required skill in your future—whether you're a doctor making observations for a patient's file, a business executive taking instructions from your CEO for an important project...or a parent jotting down notes as you meet with your child's teacher.

So, take pen in hand, get some paper, and start taking better notes...right now.

Chapter 1

Gather Your Note-taking Equipment

This chapter is short, because my note-taking system is very simple.

There are no expensive kits to send away for.

No special instruments to buy.

No complicated equipment to learn about.

No convoluted instructions you'd need a "techie" to decipher.

Just make sure you have the following materials on hand, and we're ready to go:

1. A ball point pen
2. A three-ring binder with dividers
3. Notebook paper

One more thing...

OK, it's a *little* more complicated—there's one more essential item you need before you can take effective notes:

4. An *active brain.*

Taking notes is a *participatory* activity, whether you're sitting in a lecture or reading a homework assignment. You can't expect to take grade-winning notes if the only thing that's working is your *hand.*

In fact, if you could only bring *one* of the four required items to class, you'd be better off leaving pen, paper and notebook at home.

Ready to go? Do you have everything? Your pen? Paper? Notebook? Brain? Don't worry, I'll show you how to use everything in the following chapters.

Chapter 2

Class Notes: Learning To Listen

In one of Bob & Ray's classic radio comedy sketches, Ray plays a talk-show host whose guest is Bob, president of the Slow Talkers of America, which has come to town for its annual convention. The skit goes something like this:

Ray: So, tell me, what brings you to town?

Bob: Well...the...Slow...

Ray: Talkers of America

Bob: Talkers...

Ray: Of America

Bob: Of...

Ray: America

Bob: America...

Ray: Are having their annual convention

Bob: Are...

The impatience of Ray's character is akin to what happens to *our* minds when we're sitting through a lecture. No matter how fast someone speaks, he cannot deliver information fast enough to keep our minds entirely occupied. The slow pace of orally delivered information is simply not enough to hold our attention.

That's why our thoughts literally go out the window, up to the ceiling, or ahead to Saturday night's date, completely obliterating the lecture from our brain's attention.

This problem is precisely why many businesses are paying big bucks to have their executives take courses on listening. These corporate honchos might be talented, diligent and knowledgeable about their fields, but they are not learning as much as they can from clients and co-workers. Because they never learned how to *listen.*

In fact, many experts in management and education say that listening is one of the most neglected skills in the United States. We assume that if people can *hear,* they can *listen.* But nothing could be further from the truth.

You're probably thinking, "What does all of this have to do with taking notes in class?" The answer: Everything. As I said in the previous chapter, an active brain—one that is prepared to listen and respond—is key to taking effective notes.

I'm convinced that if two students attended a lecture—one copying every word the teacher uttered but not listening to the content; the other listening closely but not taking any notes—the second student would do much better on a surprise quiz at the end of the period.

What makes a good listener *good?*

Have you ever spoken to a good listener? What was it that indicated she was paying attention to you?

- She took her eyes off you only occasionally.
- She wasn't busy formulating a reply as you were speaking.
- She asked frequent questions.

This kind of rapt attention—which you would certainly welcome from anyone sitting through one of *your* stories —is the attitude you should bring to every lecture.

And, believe it or not, note-taking will become a way for you to improve your listening and, of course, remember more of the important information your instructors deliver in class.

"Easier said than done," you sigh? Sure it is. The classroom is as warm as a steambath. The guy in front of you is playing tic-tac-toe on his arm. The view out the window is vying for your attention. And the teacher is delivering a soliloquy on the Boer War in a tone that would put Robin Williams to sleep.

Sometimes listening actively is indeed a challenge, if not virtually impossible. But there are steps you can take to make it easier.

Sit near the front of the room

Make distraction as difficult as possible by sitting as close to the instructor as you can.

Why is it the only time people seem to *want* to be in front is when they're attending a play or a concert? I've noticed that adults who attend meetings, high school or college students in lectures, even churchgoers filling up the pews, inevitably head for the *back* of the room first, as if some deadly disease were lurking on those front-row seats. While this practice gives people at meetings the opportunity to exit unnoticed, it does nothing for students —except make it harder to hear or be heard.

The farther you sit from the teacher, the more difficult it is to listen. Sitting toward the back of the room means more heads bobbing around in front of you, more students staring out the window—encouraging you to do the same.

Sitting up front has several benefits. You will make a terrific first impression on the instructor—you might very well be the only student sitting in the front row. He'll see immediately that you have come to class to listen and learn, not just take up space.

You'll be able to hear the instructor's voice, and the instructor will be able to hear *you* when you ask and answer questions.

Finally, being able to see the teacher clearly will help ensure that your eyes don't wander around the room and out the windows, taking your brain with them.

So, if you have the option of picking your desk in class, do as they say in the old spiritual: Sit right down front.

Avoid distracting classmates

The gum cracker. The doodler. The practical joker. The whisperer. Even the perfume sprayer. Your classmates may be wonderful friends, entertaining lunch companions and ultimate weekend party animals, but their quirks, idiosyncrasies and personal hygiene habits can prove distracting when you sit next to them in class.

Knuckle-cracking and note-passing are just some of the evils that can avert your attention in the middle of your biology professor's discourse on bivalves. Avoid them.

Sit up straight

Do I sound like your mother? I know you don't want to hear it, but for once she's right: To listen effectively, you must sit correctly, in a way that will let you stay comfortable and relatively still during the entire lecture. If you are uncomfortable—if parts of your body start to ache or fall asleep—your attention will inevitably wander from the instructor's words.

As the old saying goes, "The mind can retain only as much as the bottom can sustain."

Look for nonverbal clues

Studies on human behavior indicate that only a small portion of any message is delivered by the words themselves. A greater portion is transmitted by body language, facial expression and tone of voice.

I'll spend some time later in this book helping you learn how to identify the most important points of a lecture, but take advantage of the fact that the instructor—through body language, expressions and tone of voice—will already be doing that identification work for you.

Most instructors will go off on tangents of varying relevance to the subject matter. Some will be important, but, at least during your first few classes with that particular teacher, you won't be able to tell which.

Body language can be your clue.

If the teacher begins looking at the window, or his eyes glaze over, he's sending you a clear signal: "Put your pen down. This isn't going to be on the test."

On the other hand, if he turns to write something on the blackboard, makes eye contact with several students and/or gestures dramatically, he's sending a clear signal about the importance of the point he's making.

Of course, there are many exceptions to this rule. For example, my first-year calculus instructor would occasionally launch into long diatribes about his mother or air pollution, with tones more impassioned than any he used working through differential equations.

And there was the trigonometry professor I endured who would get most worked up about the damage being done to the nation's sidewalks by the deadly menace of chewing gum.

Nevertheless, learn how to be a detective...and not overlook the clues.

Ask questions often

No, you don't have to raise your hand to ask or answer questions every 90 seconds.

Being an active listener means asking *yourself* if you understand everything that has been discussed. If the answer is "no," you must ask the instructor questions at an appropriate time or write down the questions you need answered in order to understand the subject fully.

Challenge yourself to draw conclusions from what the instructor is saying. Don't just sit there letting your hand take notes. Let your *mind* do something, too. Think about the subject matter, how it relates to what you've been assigned to read and other facts you've been exposed to.

To tape or not to tape

I am opposed to using a tape recorder in class as a substitute for an active brain for the following reasons:

- *It's time-consuming.* To be cynical about it, not only will you have to waste time sitting in class, you'll have to waste more time listening to that class *again!*

- *It's virtually useless for review.* Fast-forwarding and rewinding cassettes to find the salient points of a lecture is my definition of torture. During the hectic days before an exam, do you really want to waste time listening to a whole lecture when you could just reread the material?

- *It offers no back-up.* Only the most diligent students will record *and* take notes. But what happens if your tape recorder malfunctions? How useful will blank or distorted tapes be to you when it's time to review? If you're going to take notes as a back-up, why not just take good notes?

- *It costs money.* Compare the price of blank paper and a pen to that of recorder, batteries and tapes. The cost of batteries *alone* should convince you that you're better off going the low-tech route. (Save those batteries for your Walkman.)

- When you rely on your tape-recorded lecture for garnering notes, *you miss the "live" clues* we discussed earlier. When all you have is a tape of your lecture, you don't see that zealous flash in your teacher's eyes, the passionate arm-flailing, the stern set of the jaw, any and all of which should scream, "Pay attention. I guarantee this will be on your test!"

Having spent all my fury against tape recorders, I concede that there are times they can be useful. Such as when your head is so stuffed up with a cold that "active listening" during a long lecture is virtually impossible.

Or when the material is so obtuse, you know you have to listen to it more than once just to begin to understand it.

Within the first five minutes of the first lecture of my freshman Physical Chemistry class at Princeton, I was totally lost—and I knew, even then, I would never *not* be lost. I tried tape recording the class, hoping against hope, I suppose, that listening to the monotone drone of formula after formula would somehow make more sense in the quiet of my room than it did in a classful of furiously-scratching students.

It didn't help. I understood less of the garbled formulas on tape than I did the first time I heard them. But I'll also admit that it *may* have helped someone less scientifically dense than I.

With these possible exceptions noted, I still maintain that a tape recorder will never be an ample substitute for well-developed listening skills.

Did you get that?

Okay, now that you've learned a little bit about how to listen *actively*, it's time to learn about note-taking strategies. Let's move on to the next chapter.

Chapter 3

Class Notes: Successful Strategies

Note-taking *strategies?*

What could *possibly* be so complicated about taking notes that one would need *strategies.*

After all, it's just a matter of writing down what the instructor says, isn't it? OK, maybe not verbatim, just the key stuff, but ...

If you want to take notes *effectively,* there's more to it.

As I've said before, taking down everything the teacher says is *not* an effective strategy. In fact, the most prolific note-takers might be downright *terrible* students.

You can make life easier on yourself if you follow these successful note-taking strategies--and become a *terrific* student in the process.

Come to class prepared

Remember the four ingredients of my successful note-taking program? While pen and paper are obvious, and the importance of an active brain now, I hope, equally so, why a binder?

The binder offers several advantages over composition books and spiral notebooks.

1. It allows for *easy and neat insertion and removal* of notes. If you've written down a page of notes that you later realize are useless, you can easily get rid of them.

2. More importantly, the binder allows you to *supplement and reorganize* your notes. You can—with the aid of an inexpensive hole puncher—insert handouts and pertinent quizzes, photostats of articles from periodicals and completed homework assignments near appropriate notes. Also, if instructors expand upon earlier lessons, you can place your new notes in the right place—they'll make more sense and be more useful when you review for exams and term papers.

3. The binder allows you to *travel light*—you don't even have to carry it to class; leave it home. Carry a folder with enough sheets of blank paper to classes; sort your notes and file them in your binder every night. An exercise that will take all of two minutes.

Listen first, *then* write

A young friend of mine boasted that he finished reading the book, *Green Eggs and Ham*, faster than anyone else in his second-grade class. Pleased that he had discovered one of my favorite Dr. Seuss stories, I asked him what he thought of the book. He replied, "I don't know. I was going so fast, I didn't have time to *read* it."

My friend, bright and eager as he is, had missed the point of his reading assignment. And undoubtedly, had his teacher given a **Green Eggs and Ham** test, would have scored much lower than some of the slower readers in his class.

If you find yourself furiously filling your notebook pages with your teacher's every pearly word, you might boast the most detailed notes in the class, but I doubt you will truly understand much of what you've so diligently copied.

Why are you taking notes in class?

Are you practicing to enter a speed-writing contest?

Do you want to perfect your dictation-taking skills?

Or are you hoping to actually learn something?

Listen to what your teacher is saying. Think about it. Make sure you understand it. Paraphrase it. *Then,* write your notes.

Understand the big picture

If you are actively listening, and listening before you write, then your understanding of the "big picture" (with apologies to A. Whitney Brown) ought to follow naturally.

Let's say your history teacher is rattling off dates and names of battles from the Franco-Prussian War. Your classmates in the back of the room may go into a panic as they scramble to jot down all the tongue-twisting foreign names that are being spewed out at machine gun speed.

But *you*, who are sitting up front and listening actively, pause, pen in hand, as your teacher sums up her point: that battle activity increased to a frenzy in the final months before war's end. You jot down a brief note to that effect, knowing that you can check your textbook later for all the names, dates and details of specific battles.

Your poor friends in the back, while capturing most of the battle names, missed the main point—the big picture —and now will feel compelled to memorize the list of names and dates, even though they won't know why they even copied them down in the first place.

Take notes on what you *don't* know

You *know* the first line of the Gettysburg address. You *know* the chemical formula for water. You *know* what date Pearl Harbor was bombed. So why waste time and space writing them down?

Frequently, your teachers will present material you already know in order to set the stage for further discussion, or to introduce material that is more difficult. Don't be so conditioned to write down dates, vocabulary, terms, formulas and names that you mindlessly scribble down information you already know. You'll just be wasting your time—both in class and, later, when you review your overly detailed notes.

Tailor your note-taking to class format

The extent of note-taking required—as well as the importance of those notes to your success in class—will depend to a great extent on the format of each class. There are three different types you'll need to know and adapt to:

- *The lecture.* Teacher speaks, you listen. While some high-school teachers conduct classes in this relatively impersonal way, this format is usually adapted for popular college courses, such as Geology 101 *(aka* "Rocks for Jocks"). In such situations, your teacher might never even know your name. Consequently, your note-taking and listening skills are the only tools you'll be able to use in your quest for top grades.

- ***The seminar.*** Again, more common at the college level, seminars are also known as *tutorials* or *discussion groups.* Usually conducted by graduate students, they are often held in conjunction with the larger lectures, giving students a chance to discuss the subject matter in a group of less than a hundred.

  While this format places a great deal of emphasis on your question-asking and answering skills, you should not neglect your note-taking skills. Be all ears while the discussion is flowing, but, as soon as possible *after* the class, write down the most important points discussed.

- ***Hands-on classes.*** Science and language labs, art classes and courses in industrial arts will require you to *do* something. But *while* you are doing it, remember to keep a notebook handy.

  I had a chemistry teacher who, during labs, quite often launched into extensive theoretical discussions. The less dull-witted among us quickly learned to keep our notebooks close by, capturing facts and figures he never mentioned again—except on the exams!

Observe your instructor's style

All instructors (perhaps I should say all *effective* instructors) develop a plan of attack for each class. They decide what points they will make, how much time they will spend reviewing assignments and previous lessons, what texts they will refer to, what anecdotes they will bring into the lecture to provide comic relief or human interest.

Building a note-taking strategy around each instructor's typical plan of attack for lectures is another key to academic success.

Throughout junior high school and much of high school, I had to struggle to get good grades. I took copious notes, studied them every night, pored over them before every quiz and exam.

I was rewarded for my efforts with "straight A's", but resented the hours I had to put in while my less ambitious buddies found time for a lot more fun things.

But some of the brighter kids had leisure time, too. When I asked them how they did it, they shrugged their shoulders and said they didn't know.

These students had an innate talent that they couldn't explain, a sixth sense about what to study, what were the most important things a teacher said, what instructors were most likely to ask about on tests.

In fact, when I was in a study group with some of these students, they would say, "Don't worry, she'll never ask about that." And sure enough, she never did.

What's more, these students had forgotten many of the details I was sweating. They hadn't even bothered to write any of them down, let alone try to remember them.

What these students innately knew was that items discussed during any lesson could be grouped into several categories, which varied in importance:

- Information not contained in the class texts and other assigned readings
- Explanations of obscure material within the texts and readings that students might have difficulty with
- Demonstrations or examples that provided greater understanding of the subject matter.
- Background information that put the course material in context.

As you are listening to an instructor, decide which of these categories best fits the information being presented. This will help you determine how detailed your notes on the material should be. (This will become especially easy as you get to know the instructor.)

An example that comes to mind is that of a physics professor I had, who devoted about half of every session to an examination of an important mathematician's or physicist's life and the circumstances surrounding his or her discoveries. At first, I took copious notes on these lectures, only to find that the first two exams were filled, top to bottom, with problems and formulae, not biographical questions.

Needless to say, even *I* figured out that I shouldn't take such comprehensive notes about biographical details.

Read, read, read

Most good instructors will follow a text they've selected for the course. Likewise, unless they've written the textbook themselves, most teachers will supplement it with additional information. Good teachers will look for shortcomings in textbooks and spend varying amounts of class time filling in these gaps.

As a result, it makes sense to stay one step ahead of your instructors. Read ahead in your textbook so that, as an instructor is speaking, you know what part of the lesson you should write down and what parts of it are *already* written down in your textbook. Conversely, you'll immediately recognize the supplemental material that you might need to take more detailed notes on.

Will you be asked about this supplemental material on your exams?

Of course, if you ask your teacher that question, he'll probably say something like, "You are expected to know everything that's mentioned in this class." That's why it's best to pay attention (and not ask stupid questions you already know the answers to!).

You'll quickly learn to tell from a teacher's body language what he or she considers important and what's tangential. (See Chapter 2 for more on this.)

In addition, your experience with the teacher's exams and spot quizzes will give you a great deal of insight into what he or she considers most important.

Instant replay: Review your notes

I worked for a time as a reporter on a trade magazine. I would take voluminous notes as sources were talking to me. Days later, as I reread these notes, I'd invariably discover that I really didn't have any full, direct quotes—just snatches of sentences. I couldn't write fast enough to capture the whole thing.

The solution? No, it *wasn't* a tape recorder. It was to read the notes over *immediately* after the conversation. This would allow me to fill in the blanks, putting in the words I couldn't take down at conversational speed.

You should do the same with your class notes. Take the time to look them over briefly at lunch breaks, in study halls, when you go home. Honestly evaluate whether they will be decipherable when it comes time to study for your exams. If not, add to them what you can *while your memory of the class is still fresh.*

Even as you implement these strategies, which will reduce the amount of time you're scribbling notes, you'll still find yourself in situations where you want to capture a lot of information—quickly.

I'll show you how in the next chapter.

Chapter 4

Class Notes: Shorthand Skills

"**I**f u cn rd ths msj u can ern gd py as sctry."

So went one of those vocational-training-school ads plastered in the New York City subways a few years ago. We might add, "+ u can b btr stdnt."

You don't have to be a master of shorthand to utilize helpful abbreviations for note-taking. Leaving out unnecessary vowels and articles is just one way to write quickly while taking notes—since you can mentally insert them later, why write them when you're struggling to get all of the really *important* things your instructor is saying?

On the next page is a list of standard abbreviations you will find useful in most of your classes—you may recognize many of these symbols from math or logic:

≈	*Approximately*
w/	*With*
w/o	*Without*
wh/	*Which*
→	*Resulting in*
↔	*As a result of/consequence of*
+	*And or also*
*	*Most importantly*
ff	*Following*
<	*Less than*
>	*More than*
=	*The same as, equal to*
↑	*Increasing*
↓	*Decreasing*
esp	*Especially*
Δ	*Change*
∴	*Therefore*

Expanding on your 'shorthand'

While you're listening to your instructor, you should be thinking about what you write down. Lectures are filled with so many words that will not be at all helpful when you sit down to study for the big exam. Writing all of *those* words down—while missing some of the truly important points of the lecture—is counterproductive: Your notes may look impressively complete, but what are they completely full *of*? All the important stuff, or...?

For instance, if your teacher says, "The harsh terms of the Treaty of Versailles and the ineffectiveness of the Weimar Republic were two of the most prevalent themes in the early speeches of Hitler," you could write down something like:

> Erly Hitler speeches: *hrsh
> Versailles Trty, Wmr wknss.

If the Treaty of Versailles is something that has been discussed frequently in class, you might just write "Vrs," "VS," or even "V"—it simply depends on what you will easily recognize later as meaning "Versailles" (and not "very," "victory," etc.)

Continue to abbreviate *more* as more terms become readily recognizable—in that way, the speed and effectiveness of your note-taking will increase as the school year grinds on.

I've also noticed that many students are prone to write *big* when they are writing fast and to use only a portion of the width of their paper. I guess they figure that turning over pages quickly means they are taking great notes. All it really means is that they are taking notes that will be difficult to read or use when it's review time.

Force yourself to write small and take advantage of the entire width of your note paper. The less unnecessary movement the better.

In this and the preceding chapter, I've discussed how to prepare and implement a note-taking strategy in class. Now, let's look at a sample lecture so you can practice your newly developed skills.

I hope you like comparative literature!

Hitting all the right notes

Here is part of a lecture that was one of my favorites in college. I've numbered the paragraphs here so that they can be referred to easily later.

The Comic Perspective
In Comic Novels

1   The comic perspective is one which finds its most successful expression in a presentation of contrasting methods of viewing the world. These could be categorized as that of the cynic and that of the saint. The laughter and the sense of irony that a comic work of literature can instill in its readers is a result of the clash between these methods of seeing the world.

2   If the work of literature is to be considered at all successful, its readers will surely find themselves beset with the task of sorting among the alternatives offered by the idealistic and realistic sensibilities embodied within the characters and/or the narrative voice.

3   The comic novel is one which, at last, must leave its readers experiencing its world in the way a child experiences his; with wonder, honesty, imagination and confusion.

4   If we conduct an overview of protagonists in great comic novels, we find characters who are very much like children. They are innocent, idealistic and often

naive. Moreover, authors of the great comic novels go to great lengths to deny their characters a detailed past. It is almost as if the protagonists are born fully grown into the world of the novel.

5   We can learn very few biographical details about Don Quixote. We are told only that he has filled his head with the ideals and dreams of chivalry through his incessant reading of romantic literature. Moving ahead to Dickens, we find in <u>The Pickwick Papers</u> a protagonist that the author continually denies a past. It is as if, for Dickens, the intrusion or even the introduction of the past into the present must inevitably bring with it a diminution of integrity and self-sufficiency. In fact, the only instance of Mr. Pickwick attempting to remember his past results in the protagonist falling asleep before he can do so.

6   When we get to the 20th-century comic novels we notice a continuity of this device. Paul Pennyfeather is delivered into the chaotic world of <u>Decline and Fall</u> as if from a womb. Evelyn Waugh devotes three sentences to the history of his protagonist. He is an orphan (someone who by definition cannot know his past) who "lived in Onslow Square with his guardian, who was abysmally bored by his company..."

While you don't have the luxury of being able to *hear* these words, as, of course, you would in a real lecture, pretend that you were suddenly stripped of the benefits afforded by the printed page—the ability to reread a portion of a lecture that you wouldn't be able to "rehear."

What would you come up with? How many of the actual words from the lecture would turn up in your notes? Would you be trying to get down everything the professor said?

While this lecture *sounds* eloquent, it has more sizzle to it than steak. Hence, your notes can be quite brief. Here are what mine looked like (with the paragraph references added):

Cmc Prspctv in Cmc Nvls

1. CP=2 wys seeing wrld—cynic, saint. Clash=lftr
2. Chrctrs, nrrtr embdy idlsm or rlsm
3. Rdr xprnc=chld's wrld view=cnfused, inncnt
4. Prtgnsts like chldrn—no pst
5. e.g. Dkns/pkwk, Cvnts/DonQ
6. e.g. Wgh/pnnyftr

It ain't pretty, but it works

I readily admit that reducing an instructor's eloquent words to this type of shorthand is like summarizing Lincoln's "Gettysburg Address" as:

"Many young men died in the war. What a shame. Hope it ends soon."

However, trying to capture the eloquence and missing half of the teacher's points would make much less sense.

What taking such brief notes will do is allow you to sit back, listen, and watch the instructor. This will help you capture the entire *message* that he or she is communicating, not just the *words*. If you think that the words are very important, try to elaborate on your shorthand while they are still rattling around in your head—right after the lecture. It's not a bad idea to do this anyway, especially as you start to develop your own note-taking shorthand. It'll allow you to make sure you understand your own abbreviations.

But is it good for you?

Do you think this sort of shorthand will work for you? You probably won't at first. And, in fact, you may need to radically alter it to your own specifications. But whatever system you wind up using, practice is key—as you gain more experience, your note-taking will become more and more productive.

Take a closer look at the shorthand summary in this chapter. I knew perfectly well that the abbreviations for "world" and "children" and even "narrator" would be clear to me years down the line. But abbreviating "saint" and, even more so, "cynic," I knew, would make the meaning of the notes unclear after only a short time. So in your fervor to adopt my shorthand system, don't abbreviate so much that your notes are absolutely unintelligible to you almost as soon as you write them!

The point here is, you must come up with a note-taking shorthand system that makes sense to *you*. You may certainly choose to abbreviate less, to write a little more. Whatever system you develop, just make sure it serves the same purpose: giving you the time to really *listen* to your instructors, rather than merely writing down every word they say.

Chapter 5

Texts: Read First, *Then* Write

I'm sure it's abundantly clear to all of you that not many best-selling authors moonlight writing textbooks. Most of the tomes given to you in classes—even the ones for *Literature* classes—are poorly written, badly organized cures for insomnia. Dull is the kindest word to describe all but a few of them.

That said, it's also clear that no matter how dull the prose, your job is to mine the important details from your textbooks to get good grades. Lest you have to wade through that lifeless mass of words more than once, why not take great notes the *first* time through?

You can borrow many of the strategies you implemented for taking notes in class for your attack on your reading assignments, as well. Just as you used your active brain to listen carefully to what your teacher talked about, you can use that same piece of equipment to *read* actively.

Read, then write.
Make sure you understand the big picture.
Take notes on what you don't know.

These same principles we discussed in conjunction with taking notes in class apply to taking notes on your reading materials. But there are some additional strategies you should also consider.

Change the way you read

When we read a book for pleasure, we tend to read, naturally, from beginning to the end. (Though some of us may be guilty of taking a peek at the last chapter of a suspenseful mystery novel.) Yet this linear approach, beginning at point A and moving in a direct manner to point B, is not necessarily the most effective way to read texts for information.

If you find yourself plowing diligently through your texts without having the faintest clue as to what you've read, it's time to change the way you read. The best students don't wade through each chapter of their textbooks from beginning to end. Instead, they read in an almost circular fashion. Here's how:

Look for clues

If we have curled up with the latest Stephen King thriller, we fully expect some clues along the way that will hint at the gory horror to come. And we count on Agatha Christie to subtly sprinkle keys to her mysteries' solutions long before they are resolved in the drawing room.

But most of you probably never tried to solve the mystery of your own textbooks by using the telltale signs and signals almost all of them contain. That's right—***textbooks are riddled with clues*** that will reveal to the perceptive student all the note-worthy material that must be captured. Here's where to find them:

- ***Chapter heads and subheads.*** Bold-faced headings and subheadings announce the detail about the main topic. And, in some textbooks, paragraph headings or bold-faced "lead-ins" announce that the author is about to provide finer details. So start each reading assignment by going through the chapter, beginning to end, but ***reading only the bold-faced heads and subheads.***

   This process of headline reading takes only a few minutes, but it lays the groundwork for a more intelligent and efficient reading of the chapter. You'll have some idea where the author is headed, and this will give you a greater sense of what the most important details are.

- ***End-of-chapter summaries.*** If you read a mystery from start to finish, the way the author hopes you will, you're likely to get thrown off the scent of the murderer by "red herrings" and other common detective novel devices. However, if you read the last part first, knowing the outcome would help you notice how the author constructed the novel and built an open-and-shut case for his master sleuth. You'd notice a plethora of details about the eventually unmasked murderer that might have gone unnoticed were he just another of the leading suspects.

Similarly, knowing what the author is driving at in a textbook will help you look for the important building blocks for his conclusions while you're reading.

While it may not be as much fun to read a mystery novel this way, when it comes to textbook reading and note-taking, it will make you a much more *active* reader, and, consequently, make it much less likely that you will doze off while being beaten senseless by the usual ponderous prose.

- **Pictures, graphs, charts.** Most textbooks, particularly those in the sciences, will have charts, graphs, numerical tables, maps and other illustrations. All too many students see these as mere filler—padding to glance at, then forget.

  If you're giving these charts and graphs short shrift, you're really shortchanging *yourself.* You don't have to redraw the tables in your notes, but it would be helpful to observe how they supplement the text, what points they emphasize and make note of these. This will help you put them into your own words, which will help you remember them later. And it will ensure that you don't have to continually refer to your textbooks when brushing up for an exam.

- **Highlighted terms, vocabulary and other facts.** In some textbooks, you'll discover that key terms and information are highlighted within the body text. (And I *don't* mean by a previous student; consider such yellow-swathed passages with caution—their value is directly proportional to that student's final grade, which you don't know.) Whether bold-face, italic or boxed, this is usually an indication that the material is note-worthy.

- *Questions.* Some textbook publishers use a format in which key points are emphasized by questions, either within the body or at the end of the chapter. If you read these questions *before* reading the chapter, you'll have a better idea of what material you need to pay closer attention to.

Now for the fine print

Now that you have gotten a good overview of the contents by reading the heads and subheads, reviewing the summary, picking up on the highlighted words and information and considering the review questions that may be included, you're finally ready to read the chapter.

Because you did this preliminary review first, you'll find that your reading will go much faster.

*But...*don't assume that now you can speed through your reading assignment. Okay, so Jay Leno is hosting the "Tonight Show"—for only the 84th time this year. Don't rush through your textbook, or you'll just have to read it again.

Sure, we've all heard about the boy and girl wonders who can whip through 1,000 or even 2,000 words per minute and retain it all, but most of us never will read that fast. Which is fine—it's better to read something slowly and *remember* it, than rush it into oblivion.

Many great students—even those in law school or taking umpteen courses on the 19th-century novel—never achieve reading speeds of even close to 1,000 words per minute. Some of them have to read passages they don't understand again and again to get the point.

And there's nothing wrong with that.

This is the most intelligent way to read—with *comprehension*, not speed—as your primary goal.

For a further exploration of how to read for class more effectively, I suggest you pick up a copy of ***Improve Your Reading,*** another volume in my **HOW TO STUDY** ***Program.***

Chapter 6

Texts: *Now* Get Out Your Pen

Mr. Larkin's assignment sounded simple enough: Read the photocopy of the magazine article from *Society Today* for a quiz on Friday. A fairly typical assignment that three students in the class chose to tackle in three completely different ways:

Maria read the article with her legs over the side of a sofa during a "Cheers" rerun. In this way, she missed most of the salient points in the article, though not what Norm was saying to Cliff. During commercials, however, she really hunkered down and paid close attention to what she was reading. This made Maria quite proud of herself —she usually didn't bother to read assignments at all, particularly ones as boring as this one.

Dan spent an hour at his desk on Thursday night reading the article—twice—and highlighting what he felt were the most important parts. He was confident that he had a good grasp of the material and completely understood the most important points of the article.

Candice spent about three hours going back and forth between the article and a legal pad, writing down long, complete sentences that, all told, summarized the salient points and a good many details of the article pretty well. She planned to read over the notes during the study hall she had before Mr. Larkin's class.

Who got the best grade?

Well, it doesn't take a genius to figure out that Candice is the most dedicated student. And she did get an A. Dan earned a B+. Maria was pretty happy with the C- she didn't have to work too hard for.

Who had the right approach? Candice, right?

Wrong. The answer is that old favorite of the multiple-choice test: none of the above.

"A" is *not* for effort

Even though the ends in some way justified Candice's means, the amount of effort she puts into most of her assignments also ensures that she doesn't have much of a personal life. She regularly works until 11 p.m., and puts in quite a few hours cracking the books on weekends.

Admirable?

Or overkill?

Well, then, you're thinking, why doesn't Dan have the right idea? After all, he put in only an hour and got a grade pretty darn close to Candice's.

Actually, if Dan had spent the same amount of time—but used it more wisely—he could have turned that B+ into an A...without working *harder*.

Work smarter, not harder

The right approach to Mr. Larkin's assignment lies somewhere between Dan's and Candice's. Careful reading and good notes are essential to earning good grades consistently. But taking good notes on written materials does not have to take a lot of time. With a good note-taking system, Candice could have gotten to bed an hour earlier (or caught that "Cheers" rerun herself).

Effective note-taking skills should:

- *Help you recognize* the most important points of a text
- *Make it easier* for you to understand those important points
- *Enhance your memory* of the text
- Provide a *highly efficient* way to study for your exams

Let's learn how to take better notes on this sort of material and practice doing it.

Find the main ideas, then the details

Step one in effective note taking from texts is to write down the *principle* points the author is trying to make. These main ideas should be placed either in the left-hand margin of your note paper, or as headings. *Do not write complete sentences*.

Then, write down the most important details or examples the author uses to support each of these arguments. These details should be noted under their appropriate main idea. I suggest indenting them and writing each idea on a new line, one under the other. Again, *do not use complete sentences*. Include only enough details so that your notes are not "Greek to you" when you review them.

A note-taking exercise

Let's practice these steps using the following article.

Democrats Vs. Republicans:
The Real Economy

The cornerstone of Republican economics is that the entire population benefits when the rich are permitted to retain more of their income for themselves. Former President Ronald Reagan believed the benefits enjoyed by wealthy Americans as a result of the 1981 tax cut would "trickle down" to all other citizens. Similarly, President Bush has advocated lowering the tax on capital gains. This would benefit the wealthy, who own most of the nation's assets, and, he contends, give a boost to the economy that would help everyone else, too.

The Democrats, on the other hand, contend that such a distribution of the tax burden is unfair. They think the federal government should increase taxes for wealthy citizens, and that government should spread the wealth directly through a variety of social programs.

The two sides were in a classic standoff through the 1980s. The Republicans were successful in keeping taxes on the wealthy low, while the Democrats did their best to ensure that spending on social programs stayed high. Since members from both camps thought it wise to increase military expenditures during the decade, the federal budget had nowhere to go but up.

In the budget agreement struck between Democrats and Republicans in 1990, both sides gave in a little. Taxes on the rich would increase a bit, and social, or entitlement, programs grow when the government had the money to pay the bills.

But at the heart of this compromise, which is more like a cease-fire than a treaty to end the long war, legislators face the same choices: growth or fairness, private investment or public spending, tax cuts for the wealthy or entitlement programs for the middle class and poor. In this war, the Republicans wave the flag of pure American capitalism, with its ideals of individualism and self-determination. The Democrats, some would argue, represent the kinder, gentler side of human nature (despite Mr. Bush's campaign assertions to the contrary).

But is this the real choice facing Americans in the 1990s and beyond?

Many would argue that it is not. And the reason is that both sides are wrong.

The American capitalism so dear to the Republicans is no longer dependent on the private investments of motivated, aggressive American capitalists. Future economic success in the United States depends instead on the country's unique qualities: the skills and insights of the workforce and their application to the realities of a global economy.

The Democrats are equally wrong: The role of government is not merely to spread the wealth. It is to build "human capital" and our infrastructure. More than ever, brain power, linked by roads, airports, computers, and cables, is the key factor in determining a nation's standard of living.

As you read any article, you'll notice, of course, that certain words appear repeatedly. Rather than write them down again and again during your note taking, develop an easy-to-use shorthand for the article and write a key to it across the top of the page.

For instance, in this article, the author uses several terms that can be represented as follows: R (for Republicans); D (for Democrats); E (for economy or economic); EP (for entitlement or social programs); $ (for wealth); G (for government); C (for capitalism); and T (for taxes).

Getting it all down

Here's what my notes for this text might look like:

Democrats Vs. Republicans:
The Real Economy

R=Republicans $=Wealth
D=Democrats   G=Government
E=Economy   T =Taxes
EP=Entitlement programs

(This list should, of course, be expanded as you read more of the article, so leave room to do so.)

I. R—lower T for rich=E benefits

A. Reagan—'81 T cut. "Trickle down"

B. Bush—Lower cap. gains T

II. D—More T on rich=more G EP

III. 1980s standoff—R vs. D

A. T on rich low. EP high. Budget balloons.

IV. Both sides wrong.

A. R E theory wrong. C no longer needs private investments.

B. D wrong—G must build "human capital"/infrastructure—global competitor.

Now, read the next section of this article and take notes on it using the method outlined above. Then, compare what you've written with the sample notes I've included on the page following.

Democrats Vs. Republicans:
The Real Economy
Worldwide Capital

The world economy has been changing at a whirlwind rate, and U.S. economic policy has not helped the nation prepare for 21st-century realities.

When it comes to the concept of global capital, the Republicans again have it wrong. Investments by rich Americans no longer "trickle down" to the rest of the population. Instead, they flow out into the world at large, seeking the best returns available.

At the same time, foreigners' investments seek good returns in the U.S. Overseas investments had risen to $2 trillion in 1989, an increase of 12 percent from the prior year. Since 1980, the U.S. has seen a fourfold increase in foreign capital investment. Capital moves around the world, paying little attention to borders.

Similarly, American money goes abroad as U.S. firms looking for higher profits build factories, buy equipment, and establish laboratories there. As a result, though profits earned in the U.S. by American multinational corporations fell 19 percent in 1989, foreign profits at these same firms increased by 14 percent.

Therefore, wealthy Americans might enjoy high returns from their foreign investments, but few other Americans enjoy the results. Simply put, the cohesion between American capitalists and the American economy is becoming unglued.

Applying the system

How closely do your notes resemble these?

V. Worldwide Capital

I. More $ invested abroad—no more trickle down

II. 1989: $ into U.S. up record 12% to $2 trillion. Up 400% since '80.

III. More U.S. $ goes overseas seeking more profits

IV. Corp. earnings in U.S. down 19%, up 14% abroad

V. Connection: Rich-E gone

Another exercise: What's the question?

Of course, reading in this way will make your notes that much more succinct and valuable, as will another device for making yourself a more active reader: asking yourself questions about the material. For example:

- What are the most important points in the section I've just read?

- What information from this section is my instructor likely to ask about in the next exam?

- What important theories/ideas from my other reading are covered, explained or expanded here?

As you read the text, try thinking of note-taking as just writing down the answers to questions about the material.

For instance, let's take a look at this brief excerpt from the article, "A National Care Agenda," by Suzanne Gordon, which appeared in the January 1991 edition of *The Atlantic Monthly*:

The United States is experiencing an extreme crisis in caring. As a society we cannot seem to muster the political will to care for the most precious things we produce: other human beings.

The United States has slipped to 25th place in the world in its infant-mortality rate. Twenty percent of America's children are destitute. More than 37 million people have no health insurance; 20 million to 30 million more are under-insured. Today, as patients are discharged earlier and earlier from the nation's hospitals, family members are increasingly asked to provide for their complex medical and emotional needs.

It is estimated that 1.8 million women now care for children and elders simultaneously, and 33 percent of women who care for frail elderly relatives do so in addition to holding down jobs.

Yet not only do these caregivers, who relieve our health-care system of a tremendous financial burden, receive little help; they are often penalized for providing such care, through the loss of wages or of the job itself.

Phew! The author is throwing around a lot of statistics to impress upon her readers that the United States must give some consideration to people who provide infants and older people with home health care.

Should we remember the statistics about infant mortality, inadequate health insurance, the burdens on working women? Should these statistics appear in our notes?

If we read linearly, starting at the beginning and plodding along to the last word, we probably would be tempted to write down these numbers and what they mean in our notes. But, if we were to look ahead in the article (and glance at the sub-heads), we'd find that the author is actually making a case for investments in home care by the federal government and talking about where the money should come from.

Therefore, the statistics are not especially important, but the enormity of the problem to which they give credence *is*.

A note on primary sources

Primary sources (what *Freud* said, rather than what some textbook author *says* he said) present some unique note-taking challenges.

While textbooks give you digested information, primary sources require you to do more work to get to the heart of the matter. In the sciences (social and physical), literary criticism, history and philosophy, original thinkers will present assertions and findings. They might suggest new theories or other explanations of events or phenomena. And, in doing any of the above, they will very likely support or seek to disprove established beliefs and theories.

Your notes on primary source documents should summarize the author's assertions. Under each of these summaries, you should make notes on the arguments and evidence the author presents in support of these conclusions.

The process here can be similar to that outlined above. You can first skim the document to see what the author is presenting that's truly *new* (or, at least, was new when he or she wrote it), and then go back to see how he or she proves these claims.

For instance, if you are assigned *Thus Spake Zarathustra* by Nietzsche in your Philosophy 101 course, the headings in your notes might be:

1. The dominant force in history is the "will to power."
2. A "transvaluation of values" is necessary to produce a system of morality that produces greatness rather than goodness.
3. Blending Dionysian instinct with Apollonian reason and ethics will result in the "Ubermensch" (Superman).
4. Democracy promotes conformity and suppresses excellence.
5. God is dead.

You could easily gather these by skimming the text—because of Nietzsche's tendency to use aphorisms—or by reading a good introduction to it. Then, as you read the text more thoroughly, you'd want to note how the philosopher supports these assertions.

In this chapter, I pointed out some of the components to look for when taking notes from reading assignments, and touched on one of the most important tools to help you get down the material in an organized manner. In the next, I'll give your an even more powerful tool—outlining.

Chapter 7

Texts: Outlines And Other Tools

I have a confession to make: To this very day, I resent having to write an outline for a book, article, or research project. I'd much rather just sit down and start writing.

Even though I know that doing an outline is a great way to organize my thoughts so that I can write more quickly, it just seems to take more time that I could spend actually *writing*.

Well, I would have hated myself in school if I knew then what I know now: You should do outlines while you are *reading*, as well.

Outlines will help you review a text more quickly and remember it more clearly.

And outlining texts will make you a *better* writer.

Many students underline in their textbooks or use magic markers to "highlight" them. This is a sure sign of masochism, as it guarantees only one thing: They will have to read a great deal of the deadly book again when they review for their exams.

Others write notes in the margin. This is a little bit better as a strategy for getting better grades, but marginalia usually make the most sense only in context, so this messy method also forces the student to reread a great deal of text.

What's *the* most effective way to read and remember your textbooks? *(Sigh.)* Yes, the outline.

Reverse engineering

Outlining a textbook, article or other secondary source is a little bit like what the Japanese call "reverse engineering"—a way of developing a schematic for something so that you can see exactly how it's been put together. Seeing how published authors build their arguments and marshal their research will help you when it comes time to write your own papers.

Seeing that logic of construction will also help you a great deal in remembering the book—by putting the author's points down in *your* words, you will be building a way to retrieve the key points of the book more easily from your memory.

What's more, outlining will force you to distinguish the most important points from those of secondary importance, helping you build a true understanding of the topic.

The bare bones of outlining

Standard outlines use Roman numerals (I, II, III, etc.), capital letters, Arabic numerals (1, 2, 3, 4...), and lower-case letters and indentations to show relationship and importance of topics in the text. While you certainly don't have to use the Roman-numeral system, your outline should be organized in the following manner:

Title

Author

I. First important topic in the text
    A. First sub-topic
        1. First sub-topic of A
            a. First sub-topic of 1
            b. Second sub-topic of 1
        2. Second sub-topic of A
II. The second important topic in the text

Get the idea? In a book, the Roman numerals usually would refer to chapters; the capital letters to subheadings; and the Arabic numbers and lower-case letters to blocks of paragraphs. In an article or single chapter, the Roman numbers would correspond to sub-headings, capital letters to blocks of paragraphs, Arabic numerals to paragraphs, small letters to key sentences.

What's he getting at?

We understand things in outline form. Ask an intelligent person to recount something and he'll state the main points and only enough details to make his words interesting and understandable.

The discipline of creating outlines will help you zero in on the most important points an author is making and capture them, process them, and, thereby, retain them.

Sometimes an author will have the major point of a paragraph in the first sentence. But just as often the main idea of a paragraph or section will follow some of these telltale words: therefore, because, thus, since, as a result.

When we see these words we should identify the material they introduce as the major points in our outline. The material immediately preceding and following almost always will be in support of these major points.

The outline is an extraordinary tool for organizing your thoughts and your time.

Let's practice what we're preaching

Turn to chapter 10, which is an excerpt from my own **YOUR FIRST INTERVIEW:** *Everything You Need to Know to "ACE" the Interview Process and Get Your First Job* (Career Press, 1991) and then outline it. Let's see how well you've been paying attention!

Create a time line

I always found it frustrating to read textbooks in social studies. I'd go through chapters on France, England, the Far East, and have a fairly good understanding of those areas, but have no idea where certain events stood in a global context.

To help overcome that difficulty, consider drawing a time line that you can update periodically. The time line will help you visualize the chronology and remember the relationship of key world events.

For instance, a time line for the earliest years in the history of the United States might look like this (I would suggest a horizontal time line, but the layout of this book makes reproducing it that way difficult. So here's a vertical version:

1776———The American Revolution
1783———The Articles of Confederation
1786———Shay's Rebellion
1789———Ratification of the Constitution
1791———The Federal Reserve Bank
1795———The XYZ Affair
1798———The Alien and Sedition Laws

Comparing this to other timelines in your notebook would put these events in the context of the end of the Napoleonic Era and the French Revolution.

Draw a concept tree

Another terrific device for limiting the amount of verbiage in your notes and making them more memorable is the concept tree. Like a time line, the concept tree is a visual representation of the relationship among several key facts. For instance, one might depict the system of government in the United States this way:

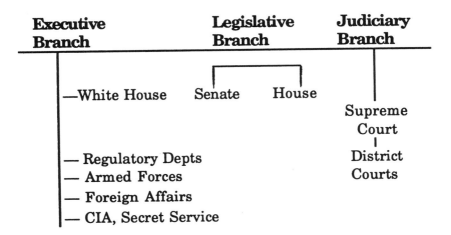

Now we can give credence to the old saying, "A picture is worth a thousand words," since time lines and concept trees will be much more helpful than mere words in remembering material, particularly conceptual material. And developing them will ensure that your interest in the text will not flag too much.

Add a vocabulary list

Many questions on exams require students to define the terminology in a discipline. Your physics professor will want to know what "vectors" are, your calculus teacher will want to know about "differential equations," your history professor will want you to be well versed on "The Cold War," and your English Lit professor will require you to know about the "Romantic Poets."

Therefore, as you read your textbook, be sure to write down all new terms that seem important and their definitions. I used to draw a box around terms and definitions in my notes, because I knew these were among the most likely items to be asked about and the box would always draw my attention to them when I was reviewing.

Most textbooks will provide definitions of key terms. However, if you look back to the article on economics we studied in Chapter 6, you'll see that the author did *not* explicitly state a definition of the "trickle-down" theory, for example, but that it *could* be inferred from the text.

This is an important point: Even if your textbook does not define a key term, make sure you write the term down in your notes *with* a definition. It will be much harder months later to remember what the term means.

In addition, even if the author does provide a definition, your notes should reflect *your* understanding of the term. Take the time to rephrase and write it in your own words. This will help you remember it.

I would also recommend writing down examples for terms that you might have trouble remembering. If you're reading an English textbook and you come across the term "oxymoron," which is defined by the author as "a figure of speech combining seemingly contradictory expressions," wouldn't it be better if your notes on figures of speech read something like this?

oxymoron:	jumbo shrimp, cruel kindness
onomatopoeia:	PLOP, PLOP, FIZZ, FIZZ
metaphor:	food for thought
simile:	this is *like* that

Wait, you're not done yet

After you've finished making notes on a chapter, go through them and identify the most important points, which are the ones that might turn up on tests, either with an asterisk or by highlighting them. You'll probably end up marking about 40 to 50 percent of your entries. When you're reviewing for a test, you should *read* all of the notes, but your asterisks will indicate which points you considered the most important while the chapter was very fresh in your mind.

To summarize, when it comes to taking notes from your texts or other reading material, you should:

- Take a cursory look through the chapter before you begin reading. Look for subheads, highlighted terms and summaries at the end of the chapter to give you a sense of the content.

- Read each section thoroughly. While your review of the chapter "clues" will help your understanding of the material, you should read for comprehension rather than speed.

- Make notes immediately after you've finished reading, using the outline, time line, concept tree and vocabulary list methods of organization as necessary.

- Mark with an asterisk or highlight the key points as you review your notes.

The advice in this chapter will help you remember the books that you have to carry back and forth to school all too often. Believe it or not, that's a luxury. When you have term papers to do, you'll be forced to use books that you cannot remove from the library.

The next chapter will tell you how to make sure you get all of the necessary information from them with the fewest trips to the stacks.

Chapter 8

Notes On Library Materials

Sometime during your high school or college years, you will undoubtedly be called upon to do some extensive research, either for a term paper or some other major project. Such a task will indeed be a major undertaking. And note-taking will be only one aspect of the process, albeit an important one.

While I will give you a terrific system for taking notes for a term paper or report in this chapter, I urge you to also read **Write Papers,** another helpful book in my **HOW TO STUDY** *Program,* which thoroughly covers *all* the important steps, from selecting a topic and developing an outline to researching and taking notes to writing, rewriting and proofreading your final paper.

As you will discover, writing a term paper will require you to take notes from a number of sources, most of them available at the library. But the more periodicals, reference books and even microfiche you uncover as terrific sources of information for your project, the more likely you'll be told you won't be able to take much of this material out of the library. You'll have to take your notes *at the library,* not at your leisure in the comfort of your room.

So you'll definitely want a note-taking system that is quick, thorough, efficient and precludes the necessity of having to return to the source *again.* What's the answer?

No, it's not photocopying.

While technology should provide convenience, it should never become a substitute for skill. Calculators should make it easier to add and divide and multiply, but we should never forget how to perform these functions without them.

Likewise, photocopying machines should make it easy for us to reproduce extensive passages from books and journals, but they should never be thought of as a substitute for taking good notes.

The reasons are similar to the arguments against tape-recording lectures that we made in Chapter 1. Photocopying does not save time, it only ensures that you will have to read materials again to unearth the most important facts from them.

Photocopying: Why it's redundant

You've found a resource that's perfect for your term paper. Your first impulse might be to find the library photocopying machine and pumping some quarters into it.

Is photocopying a help or a hindrance?

I used to employ a "system" of photocopying when preparing for my term papers. I would go to the library with nothing except a roll of dimes (photocopying was a lot cheaper in those days), and comb the card catalog, the stacks, and the periodicals index for possible sources, using the library-supplied pencils to write the information down on call slips. I'd stack the volumes and periodicals around me at one of the tables and comb through them for hours, looking for juicy quotes and fun factoids.

I'd mark the books with those handy call slips. Then, I'd haul all of the useful sources over to the photocopier and begin pumping away my hard-earned money.

I'd wind up going home with a pile of photostats that I had to read (and, as for the material, *reread*), which I'd do armed with pens of as many different colors as I could find. I'd underline all of the related passages with the same color, pick up another pen and go sifting through the photocopies again. This method certainly helped me produce some darn good papers, but it also ensured that I spent too much time researching, rereading information, organizing and reorganizing the research before I ever began actually writing.

I'm about to save you a lot of grief by letting you in on one of the greatest card tricks you've ever seen. And, by the way, you won't ever have to wait in line for the photocopying machine at the library again.

Become a "poINDEXter"

When I was in school, we called the smart kids "Poindexters." (You probably call them "nerds.") Well, the root of Poindexter is *index*, and the smart kids' secret to writing effective term papers with the least effort, it just so happens, was index cards.

While that metaphor was a bit of a stretch, it's not an exaggeration to say that index cards will cut the time it takes to research and organize a term paper in half.

Here's how they work:

As you'll learn when you read **Write Papers,** developing a preliminary outline is an important early step in the paper-writing process. Assuming you have completed this step, you would then be prepared to gather information for your term paper or research project. Proceed to your local stationery store and buy a supply of 3-by-5 note cards.

As you review each source, you'll discover some are packed with helpful information, while others may have no useful material at all. Once you determine that you will use a source, make a working bibliography card:

- *In the upper right-hand corner of the card*: Write the library call number (Dewey decimal or Library of Congress number), or any other detail that will help you locate the material (e.g., "Science Reading Room," "Main Stacks, 3rd Floor," etc.).

- *On the main part of the card:* Write the author's name, if one is given, last name first. Include the title of the article, if applicable, and write and underline the name of the book, magazine or other publication. In addition, include any other details, such as date of publication, edition, volume number or page numbers where the article is found.

- *In the upper left-hand corner:* Number the card—the card for the first source you plan to use, for example, is #1; the second, #2, and so on. If you accidently skip a number or end up not using a source for which you've filled out a card, don't worry. It's only important that you assign a different number to each card.

- ***At the bottom of the card:*** Write the name of the library (if you're working at more than one) at which you found the source.

By filling out a card for each source, you have just created your ***working bibliography***—a listing of all your sources, which will be an invaluable tool when you have to prepare the final bibliography for your term paper.

Sample Bibliography Card For A Book

```
(1)                               315.6
                        Main Reading Room

        Jones, Karen A.

The Life and Times of Bob Smith.
        (see esp. pp. 43-48)


              Card Catalog
           Main Street Library
```

Sample Bibliography Card For A Magazine Article

```
(2)                    Periodical Room

            Perkins, Stan
 "The Life and Times of Bob Smith"
          Smith Magazine
     (April 24, 1989; pp. 22-26)


            Readers' Guide
          University Library
```

Sample Bibliography Card
For A Newspaper Article

```
(3)                          Microfiche Room

              Black, Bill
   "Bob Smith: The New Widget Spinner"
           New York Times
   (June 16, 1976, late edition, p. A12)

          New York Times Index
          Main Street Library
```

Okay, so why the card game?

With index cards, you can organize your list of resources in different ways, just by shuffling the deck.

For example, you might want to start by organizing your cards by resource: magazine articles, encyclopedias, books, newspapers, etc. Then, when you're in the magazine room of the library, you will have a quick and easy way to make sure you read all your magazine articles at the same time. Ditto for your trip to the newspaper reading room, the reference shelf, and so on.

But at some point, you might want to have your list of resources organized in alphabetical order. Or separated into piles of resources you've checked, and those you haven't. No problem: Just shuffle your cards again.

Even with the help of a computer, it would be time-consuming to do all of this on paper. The note-card system is neater and more efficient. And that's the key to getting your work done as quickly and painlessly as possible!

Now, for taking notes

You're sitting in the library, now, surrounded by a veritable bonanza of source materials for your paper. You've completed your bibliography cards. It's time to take notes. Here's how:

- **Write one thought, idea, quote or fact—and only *one*—on each card.**

  No exceptions. If you encounter a very long quote or string of data, you can write on both the front and back of the card, if necessary. But *never* carry over a note to a second card. If you have an uncontrollable urge to do that, the quote is too long. If you feel that the author is making an incredibly good point, paraphrase it.

- **Write in your own words.**

  Don't copy material word for word—you may inadvertently wind up plagiarizing when you write. Summarize key points or restate the material in your own words.

- **Put quotation marks around any material copied verbatim.**

  Sometimes an author makes a point so perfectly, so poetically, you *do* want to capture it exactly as is. It's fine to do this on a limited basis. But when you do so, you must copy such statements *exactly*—every word, every comma should be precisely as written in the original. And make sure you put quotation marks around this material. Don't rely on your memory to recall, later, which copy was paraphrased and which you copied verbatim.

- *Put the number of the corresponding bibliography card in the upper-left corner.*

    This is the number you put in the upper-left-hand corner of the bibliography card.

- *Include the page numbers (where you found the information) on the card.*

    You can add this information under the resource number.

- *Write down the topic letter that corresponds to your preliminary outline.*

    For example, the second section, "B," of your preliminary outline is about the French withdrawal from Viet Nam. You find an interesting quote from a United States official that refers to this withdrawal. Write down the topic letter "B" in the upper right-hand corner of your note card. (If you're not sure, mark the card with an asterisk [*] instead. Later, when you have a more detailed outline, you may discover where it best fits.)

- *Give it a headline.*

    Next to the topic letter, add a brief description of the information on the card. For example, your note card with the quote about the French withdrawal may read, "French Withdrawal: U.S. Comments."

As you fill out your note cards, be sure to transfer information accurately. Double-check names, dates and other statistics. The beauty of using the note-card system is that, once you've captured the information you need, you should never have to return to any of the sources a second time.

A note of caution here: While this system is terrific for helping you organize your time and material, don't allow it to hamstring you if you find other interesting material.

For instance, you might come across interesting quotes or statistics that could add flavor and authority to your term paper, but you're not quite sure where they will fit in. Put an asterisk on the card; return to it later.

As with the other exercises in note-taking, the index card system requires you not to be a *copyist*—you could have used the photostat machine for that—but a *processor of information.*

Constantly ask yourself questions while looking at the source material:

- ***Is the author saying this in such a way that I want to quote her directly, or should I just paraphrase the material?***

   If you decide to paraphrase, you obviously don't have to write down the author's exact verbiage, and, therefore, can resort to some of the note-taking tips discussed in other chapters. The answer to this question, in other words, will have a big impact on how much time it takes to fill in each index card.

- ***Does this material support or contradict the arguments or facts of another author?***

   Which one of them do I believe? If there *is* contradictory evidence, should I note it? Can I refute it? If it supports the material I already have, is it interesting or redundant?

- ***Where does this material fit into my outline?***

   Often, source material won't be as sharply delineated as your plan for the term paper, which is why it is important to place *one and only one* thought on each card. Even though an author might place more than one thought into a paragraph, or even a sentence, you will be able to stick to your organizational guns if you keep your cards close to the outline vest.

Index cards make organization easy

Before I came up with any term-paper research system in high school, my student life was, quite literally, a mess. I had pages and pages of notes for term papers, but sometimes I was unsure where quotes came from and whether or not they were direct quotes or paraphrases.

My photocopy "system" wasn't much of an improvement. Often, I would forget one piece of the bibliographic information I needed, necessitating yet another last-minute trip to the library. And organizing the voluminous notes when it came time to put my thoughts in order was worse than the researching and writing itself.

The card system will save you all of that grief. Writing one thought, idea, quote, etc. per card will eliminate the problems caused when disparate pieces of information appear on the same piece of paper. And writing the number of the source down before doing anything else will help you avoid any problems relating to proper attribution.

When you're ready to do your final outline, all you'll need do is organize and reorder your cards until you have the most effective order.

This simple note-card system is, in fact, one that many professional writers—including this one—swear by long after they leave the world of term papers and class reports behind.

Chapter 9

Taking Great Notes For Oral Reports

The English poet John Donne wrote, "Death be not proud," and no wonder: In many public opinion polls in which respondents were asked to rate their biggest fears, public speaking—and *not* the good old grim reaper—won, hands down.

This leads one to wonder why there haven't been more horror films made about standing up in front of an audience than about ax murderers. And makes anyone who has done a considerable amount of public speaking wonder why more people simply don't do the sensible thing to overcome their fear of "lecternship"—prepare.

Researching, taking and properly using notes, and rehearsing, should ensure that you will have nothing but a mild case of the butterflies before you have to get up in front of your classmates, professors, or any other audience, friendly or otherwise.

Good notes are your lifeline when you stand up to say what's on your mind. They should act as cues to remind you where your talk should go next, and they should make you feel secure that you can get through the ordeal.

However, notes can also be a crutch that guarantee not success, but audience boredom. You've probably seen any number of people get up in front of an audience and just read some papers they have in front of them.

Is there any *better* cure for insomnia?

I'd just like to say a few words

Exactly what sort of talk is this going to be? Odds are, if you've been assigned to give a talk for a class, it will fall into one of the following categories:

- *Exposition*—a rather straightforward statement of facts.

- An *argument,* with which you are trying to change the opinions of at least a portion of the audience.

- A *description* which will provide a visual picture to your listeners.

- *Narration*—or story-telling.

The most common forms of oral reports assigned in school will be the exposition and argument. You'll find that you will research and organize your information for these types of speeches pretty much the way you would a straightforward term paper. So, review Chapter 8 (and, again, read *Write Papers,* one of the other four books in my HOW TO STUDY *Program*).

A note of caution: If you're preparing an *argument*, don't convince yourself you don't have to research *both* sides of the topic just because you're only presenting *one* of them. You should be doubly prepared with all the facts, as you might be challenged with questions or the arguments of other speakers.

As you gather information for your report, making notes on index cards as you did for your term paper, keep this in mind: In order for you to be effective, you must use some different techniques when you *tell* your story rather than *write* it. Here are a few:

- ***Don't make your topic too broad.*** This advice, offered for preparing written reports as well, is even more important when preparing a talk. Try giving an effective speech on "Drugs," "Hamlet" or "Capital Punishment"...in 15 minutes, frequently the amount of time assigned for oral reports. These topics are more suited to a series of books!

  "How Shakespeare portrays Hamlet As The Mad Prince" or "Why Drugs Should (or Shouldn't) Be Legalized" or "Why Capital Punishment Is No Deterrent" are more manageable. Narrowing the scope of your talk will help you research and organize it more effectively.

- ***Don't overuse statistics.*** While they're very important for lending credibility to your position, too many will only weigh down your speech and bore your audience--as anyone who sat though one of the last presidential debates can tell you.

- *Anecdotes add color and life to your talk.* But use them sparingly, because they can slow down your speech. Get to the punch-line before the yawns start.

- *Be careful with quotes.* Unlike a term paper, a speech allows you to establish yourself as an authority with less fear of being accused of plagiarism. So you can present a lot more facts without attribution. (But you'd better have the sources in case you're asked about your facts.) You can use quotes, though, when they contain distinctive language or elicit an emotion. Be sure to attribute the source.

Organizing your talk: Some free advice

I've done so much public speaking throughout my career that I've actually grown to enjoy it—in fact, I look forward to talking to a room full of strangers. I don't think that would be the case at all were it not for a piece of valuable advice I acquired quite a few years ago:

There is only one best way to organize a speech: Tell them what you are going to say; say it; then, tell them what you said.

An outline for a speech is going to be different than one for a term paper, because of the way effective presentations must be organized. Unlike readers, your listeners will not have a piece of paper in front of them to ponder and review. Your classmates and teacher will be relying on ear and memory to make sense of your talk, so you will have to be somewhat repetitious, though, hopefully, in a barely noticeable way.

When organizing your facts for your talk, you can use the same method—the index cards—as you used in preparing your term paper. But as you put together your outline, follow my advice: Tell them what you're going to say, say it, then tell them what you said. It's that simple.

Create your outline

Now that you have the information and colorful quotes you need to make a convincing speech, start organizing it. Go through your cards and decide the best way to arrange them so that they build toward a convincing argument. Then, using the order you've established, go through the cards and develop an outline.

Let's say you were assigned to take one side of the argument, "Should drugs be legalized?" Your outline might look like this:

The Opening

   I. Drugs should be legalized

  II. This will help solve, not deepen, the drug crisis in this country

III. Keeping drugs illegal assures that criminals get rich and government funds get wasted

The Middle

   I. The reasons to legalize drugs

     A. Artificially inflated prices

        1. Costs are inflated 2,500 percent

     B. Public funds are being wasted

        1. Law enforcement is not working

        2. Funds for rehabilitation are paltry

        3. Education funds are inadequate

II. Control would be easier

    A. It has worked in other countries

    B. Licensing would increase revenues

    C. Harsh penalties would curb sales to minors

    D. Drug addicts would be known and available for counseling

III. Prohibition doesn't work

    A. Parallels with Roaring Twenties

The Closing

  I. The costly, ineffective War on Drugs

  II. Legalization sounds radical, but it would work

  III. The alternative is far more dangerous

As you can see, the speech will restate the same points three times as a way of emphasizing them and assuring that they will be remembered.

Boil it down

Now read through it several times. Read it to yourself to make sure you haven't left out any important facts or arguments. Then read it aloud to see how it flows, fixing as necessary.

Now, it's time to go without a net. Stand in front of the mirror and try giving the speech, start to finish, looking at nothing but your own beautiful face. But have your notes close by.

How did you do? What parts of the speech did you remember with no trouble? Where did you stumble? If you're like 99 percent of the human race, you probably had to wrench your eyes from the mirror now and then to look at your notes.

Of course, you're not ready for an audience yet. Nor should you expect to be at this point. You'll want to practice many more times before you face your listeners. The purpose of this exercise is to help you identify what areas you really know—and which you need more prompting on.

Your next step is to distill your talk even further on additional note cards. For those areas that you're familiar with and remember without looking at your notes, jot down a simple phrase, even a symbol, that prompts you to continue with your talk. For those details you're a little unsure of, write as much detail as you need. As you continue to practice speaking, you should further distill the information on your note cards, until what you have is the barest framework possible.

My advice for preparing your final note cards is much like the advice that veteran travelers offer on packing for a long trip: Put only the bare necessities in your suitcase. Then, take half of them out.

Sounds scary, doesn't it?

It certainly did to me at one time. I took a course on public speaking at the American Management Association, one of the leading providers of continuing adult education. Since I made my living with printed words, I wanted to have lots of them in front of me so I wouldn't feel naked. I'd hide behind my legal pad!

But the instructor, to whom I've been grateful countless times since, would allow us to bring only three index cards for a three-minute talk. And each card could have no more than 10 words written on it.

Certainly many students in the class stumbled, but they probably hadn't rehearsed. On the other hand, I guarantee you that, as a relative novice at public speaking, you will make one (and maybe all) of these big mistakes if you bring your entire text with you:

- You will read from it, failing to make eye contact with your audience. This will help to ensure that you lose *their* interest and *your* credibility. How familiar can you be with a subject if you have to *read* your entire speech?

- If you stop reading for a second to ad-lib or look at your listeners, you will lose your place. It's much harder to find that key word that will jog your memory on a full page of text than on an index card.

- You won't be familiar enough with your speech, because, after all, you'll have it there with you, so why bother rehearsing or memorizing anything?

As I've become more polished as a public speaker, I've noticed that having only the cards has encouraged me to ad-lib more. And, by and large, these are the most well received parts of the speech. Talking relatively freely, with the help of only the sparest notes, is one way to make sure the "real you" comes through.

And that's who the audience is there to hear, right?

Please take note

I've begun to think of my notes for speeches as the purest form of the craft we've described in this book. You are distilling ideas down to a phrase, a word, a number, perhaps a symbol that will help you remember under pressure.

Often, the very *process* of taking notes is enough, in itself, to ensure that a fact, an impression or a formula, will last in your memory for a long time. Note-taking is stripping data down to its essence.

Although I've made many suggestions about the best way to take notes, remember that it is a very individualistic and pragmatic art. Each of you should figure out what works best for you, then refine your technique using the suggestions made in these chapters. It will be worth the effort.

In the next chapter, I've reproduced an excerpt from one of my other books—***Your First Interview***—on which to practice your newly mastered note-taking and outlining skills. And I've shown my own outline of the chapter, too. Just don't peek at my notes before you take your own!

Chapter 10

Let's Practice What We've Preached

Starting on the next page, I've reprinted an excerpt (about half of chapter 4) from my book *Your First Interview*. (I figured I might as well include an exercise on a topic in which I expect most of you are *really* interested.)

Practice outlining it (see chapter 7) and taking notes on it. You'll soon see how well you learned the lessons of this book—or what chapters you need to go back and reread!

On pages 90 and 91, I've given you two blank pages to fill in your outline. On page 92, I've reproduced my own. (Don't peek until you finish yours!) See how close you get to this "model" (though it's certainly not the only "solution").

If you find you have a lot of trouble with this exercise, forget what I said about linear reading—go back and read *Take Notes* again, from start to finish!

Not The Spanish Inquisition!
What To Expect During Your First Interview

For employers, interviewing has made the transition from art to science.

A long-time subscriber to journals for personnel *(aka* human resources) executives, I've lately seen a plethora of articles extolling the virtues of such things as "database interviews," "situational interviews," and "stress (confrontational) interviews."

While these techniques each have their own nuances, they have been developed with one goal in mind: to more accurately and reliably measure how a candidate will perform on the job if hired.

Test-tube babies

Like scientists, interviewers are now expected to gather similar types of information on all the specimens they study—information that can be measured, quantified, and more easily and accurately compared. In fact, sometimes it seems as if quantification has replaced *qualification* in the hiring process.

The reasons are not as much Orwellian as economic. The "cost of hire"—the amount of money it takes to land a suitable candidate for a job—has escalated dramatically and will continue to increase as a result of the baby bust and the much ballyhooed shrinkage of the work force.

In addition, lawsuits against employers for wrongful discharge and other employment-related causes have increased exponentially over the past decade, making it more important for companies to hire people they (hope they) won't want to get rid of.

And, last but not least, for companies in our new Service Economy, the human resource is unquestionably the most valuable in their inventories.

Not to make you more nervous than you probably already are, but for all of these reasons, interviewing is going to get tougher and tougher for job candidates at *all* levels of experience. You probably will have to go through more interviews than your predecessors—whatever job you are after, whatever your level of expertise—as well as tests designed to measure your honesty, intelligence, mental health and blood toxicity.

The screening interview

If you're going for a job at a mid-size or large company (any organization of more than about 250 employees), your first interview will often be with an employment manager in the personnel department.

More and more often, this interview is taking candidates by surprise. Why? Because many companies have begun conducting the initial screening interview by phone in an effort to save time and/or do more with less staff.

Therefore, since this will probably not be scheduled in advance, you must begin preparing for the telephone interview as soon as you send out your resumes and letters.

The scene could go something like this: You're sitting at home having your orange juice on a warm summer day three weeks after graduation. The phone rings. You saunter over to answer it, casting sidelong glances at the headlines on the morning newspaper and scratching your stomach.

"Hello," you groan.

"Good morning," says the almost too chipper voice on the other end. *"This is Molly Joyce*

of ABC Widget. I'm looking for Joseph Lerman.

"Speaking."

"Oh, hello. May I call you Joseph? You applied for our opening in the solid waste management department, and I'm calling to ask you some preliminary questions."

You're about to freeze. You gulp almost audibly. Your head swims in a rush of adrenaline. You begin looking for a way out. You consider saying, *"Oh, you want Joseph Lerman. I'm afraid he's not here right now. Can I take a message?"*

But you think better of it. and it's a good thing. After all, on the other end of the phone is not a great white shark, but Molly Joyce, recruitment manager at ABC Widget. Let's take a look at who she is and why she's calling you.

Molly is a lower-level person in the personnel department who has been trained in some fairly basic interview techniques. Odds are that she hasn't been out of college much longer than you, and she has only a bare-bones idea of the duties and responsibilities of the position for which you've applied.

Her job has a rather simple goal: reduce the number of bona fide candidates for an opening before any of them get a chance to even walk in the door.

After you've gotten through the preliminaries with Molly, her end of the conversation will follow a script—she will be asking questions to see if you have the easily quantifiable qualifications for the position—the right degree, command of the English language, the right types of internships, willingness to relocate, whatever.

Primarily, Molly will be trying to determine if you've been truthful on your resume.

The interview will also be somewhat qualitative: How well have you responded to her surprise phone call? And how quickly did you recover from the shock? Do you exhibit sufficient enthusiasm for the position? Do you exhibit any obvious emotional disturbances? How articulate are you? How energetic? How prepared? Should she or anybody else at Widget go out on a limb and recommend you for a *job?*

Okay, you know what Molly wants

So let her have it: *"Oh, Ms. Joyce, I'm so glad you called. What can I do for you this morning?"*

You've shown enthusiasm and a willingness to be co-operative. Since Molly might have 25 of these calls to do today, she'll be very grateful to you for making her job easier and more pleasant.

Remember, the telephone interview is a screening *out,* not a screening *in* process. Molly is trying to *reduce* the number of in-person interviews she, her supervisor, and the hiring manager will have to conduct.

In other words, Molly desperately wants to scratch *24* of the (25) candidates she calls today off her list. In order to beat *these* odds:

- Make it easy for Molly to get hold of you or leave messages. Buy an answering machine if there is any time during business hours that your phone might not be answered.

- Be cheerful and enthusiastic without being phony about it. Remember to smile while you're speaking on the phone.

- Be prepared. Keep a copy of your resume and cover letter and some basic facts about ABC Widget and the other companies you've applied to right by the telephone.

- Stay in control. If you don't have documents near the phone, if you're in your underwear and the doorbell has just rung, ask Molly to hold on a few seconds or offer to call her right back. Do it calmly and don't think you'll put her off. She knows she's caught you by surprise.

- Rephrase Molly's questions and repeat them back to her. This will give you time to think over your reply.

- Make sure you ascertain the correct spelling of Molly's name, her complete title and the address of the company office she works in. You should follow up the telephone interview with a letter thanking her for calling and reaffirming your interest in the job.

- Don't volunteer anything. The telephone interviewer is out to get facts and assess the truthfulness of your application. Something you might volunteer could be a reason for rejection. If you abruptly switched majors, entered and left graduate school, resigned from an internship or part-time job, let Molly ask before you tell. Tell the truth when she *does* ask, but don't feel the need to unburden yourself if she *doesn't*.

The live, in-person screening interview

Let's face it, the deck is stacked against you when Molly calls. She wants to speak once and *only* once to as many people that day as possible. It's more difficult to put your best foot forward over the telephone. And, if the company is not in a remote location, it probably is using telephone screening because so many apparently qualified candidates applied for the position. Yes, that's right. You're not the only one to hear about that terrific job at ABC Widget. In fact, you're one of 200!

On the other hand, the live screening interview gives you a better chance to make a good impression, and probably is an indication that there is a relatively small cadre of candidates or that your application is held in at least relatively high regard.

That's the good news. The bad news is that the live, and usually longer, interview gives Molly the chance to use *all* of the interview techniques she's learned and practiced.

She'll also have a chance to pass judgment on more than your words and the sound of your voice. She'll be, as the pessimists might put it, watching you squirm.

Given the fact that you have no experience, you don't fit in with the basic theory of interviews. The zealous screening interviewer, therefore, will be trying to ferret out information about your college performance, your personality, your personal interactive style that will be predictive of "future performance."

As a new kid on the block, you are making their job a little more difficult to do well, or to do as scientifically. They might not like that, and might be more tempted to try out hypothetical questions, stress techniques, and other means to get at the real you.

A track record would obviate the need for this type of performance test.

This might seem awfully complicated. Remember, personnel professionals are usually the only people at a company trained in sophisticated interviewing techniques. But then, as we'll see in the next chapter, hiring managers offer their own challenges!

Your Outline of This Chapter

_____

_____

_____

_____

_____

_____

_____

_____

_____

_____

_____

_____

_____

_____

_____

_____

_____

_____

_____

_____

_____

_____

My Outline of This Chapter

Interviewing

INT= interview   EC= economy   RS = resume

I. INT Trend: Shft Emphs—"art" to science
  A. Goal: Acctly measure cand pot
  B. Why? EC
    1. Cost of hire up (will cont.)
    2. Desire to kp empl (lawsuits up)
    3. Serv. EC (people imp)
  C. Result: Tougher INTs

II. Scrning INT: Phone
  A. Why? Saves time
    1. Lwr lvl persnnl empl
    2. Goal: rdc # cands
  B. What lkng 4?
    1. Qualifs
    2. Truth on RES
  C. Yr Goal: STAY ON LIST
    1. Shw enthsiasm
    2. Make easy to rch u
    3. Hv RS, cvr ltr, co info handy
    4. Mntn cntrl, hold 2 +gain composure
    5. Rephrs, repeat ?s
    6. Get prsn's nm, title, snd T-Y ltr
    7. Don't vlntr info, esp neg.

III. Live scrning INT
  A. Positive
    1. Chance to mk strng imprssion
    2. < cands left
  B. Negative
    1. Guinea pig for INT tchnqs
    2. Add "sight" to sound (tel)
    3. Digging for info
    4. Unhappy y'r new

Table of Contents

Ron Fry's HOW TO STUDY Program

Take Notes

Career Press

America's Premiere Publisher of books on:

- Study Skills
- Career & Job Search Advice
- Education
- Business "How-To"
- Financial "How-To"
- Careers in Advertising, Book Publishing, Magazines, Newspapers, Marketing & Sales, Public Relations, Business & Finance, the Travel Industry, Healthcare, Radio & Television and much, much more.

If you liked this book, please write and tell us!

And if you'd like a copy of our FREE catalog of nearly 100 of the best career books available, please call us (Toll-Free) or write!

THE CAREER PRESS
180 Fifth Ave.,
PO Box 34
Hawthorne, NJ 07507
(Toll-Free) 1-800-CAREER-1 (U. S. only)
201-427-0229
FAX: 201-427-2037